St. Peter: The Life and Legacy of Christ's Most Important Disciple

By Gustavo Vazquez Lozano and Charles River Editors

Marco Zoppo's depiction of St. Peter

About Charles River Editors

Charles River Editors is a boutique digital publishing company, specializing in bringing history back to life with educational and engaging books on a wide range of topics. Keep up to date with our new and free offerings with this 5 second sign up on our weekly mailing list, and visit Our Kindle Author Page to see other recently published Kindle titles.

We make these books for you and always want to know our readers' opinions, so we encourage you to leave reviews and look forward to publishing new and exciting titles each week.

Introduction

Murrillo's painting of St. Peter

St. Peter

"And Jesus suffered no man to follow Him, save Peter and James and John." – Mark 5:37

Apart from Jesus, there is no character more vividly presented in the gospels than Peter. To talk of Saint Peter is to talk about a man of action. There is a good reason why he is the apostle with the most mentions in the Gospels, and the most referred to in the New Testament (a total of 195 times). In comparison, John, the next most popular disciple, barely reaches 29 references. It is at decisive moments which require a categorical reaction where the leader of the Twelve shines; it is then that Peter —born as Simon Bar-Jonah— has no rival in the inner circle of disciples that followed Jesus of Nazareth. At the same time, during periods of uncertainty and inaction he hesitates, collapses, and shows his all-too human side. With all his virtues and shortcomings, he became Jesus´s man of confidence, and over time, the leader of the nascent Church.

Reconstructing the biography of Simon the Galilean requires throwing the nets over the waters of the many traditions of the leader of the Twelve, the man who is always present at the turning points of the story of Jesus. It has rightly been said that the Gospel of Mark (and thus the gospels of Matthew and Luke) is written from his point of view. It is he whom Jesus calls first when he is working on the seashore; it is Peter who proclaims with blind enthusiasm that his teacher is the Messiah, who confronts him about the consequences and meaning of that title, who cries bitterly for his cowardice, who enters the house of the high priest where the rabbi is held prisoner, and who, after the crucifixion, throws himself into the dark waters, before the sunrise, when he sees him again standing on the shore of the lake.

Peter was already a married man with a permanent job in Capernaum when Jesus passed by and said, "Follow me and I will make you a fisher of men." Although the four canonical gospels tend to have disagreements, they all agree on one crucial aspect: Peter's preeminence. Peter was the spokesman and the chief apostle, the trustworthy disciple of the Lord and, ironically, the one who failed him again and again through his incomprehension, his hesitation, and impulsiveness. For example, he drew the sword to kill at a time of danger, when his teacher was clearly against violence. However, according to several independent sources, the risen Jesus went to appear to Peter first, as if to comfort him and confirm him on his commission to "feed the sheep."

The primacy of the impetuous fisherman was never in doubt in the early Church. After that tragic Easter celebration where the dream seemed to come to an end, the leader of the Twelve was the first man to go outside, identify himself as a follower of the rebel who had been crucified, and start preaching courageously. Therefore, he set in motion the most vibrant Church in the world.

Considering all this, it is strange that few details about his later life are known. That Simon Bar-Jonah "Cephas," the man from Galilee, was a historical figure is a fact that no one - not even those who doubt the existence of Jesus - would put in doubt. The textual evidence is traced back to the years he lived in Jerusalem, and at least one contemporary person mentions an encounter with him. But the details are scarce. Ironically, most of the reliable information is in the writings of another Christian leader with whom he had disputes: Paul.

Traditions and legends about the life of Saint Peter are many, not to mention several writings attributed to him. Some may contain historical memories, and others are parables, but it is not a legend that while he was alive, and even 2,000 years later, Peter has been the center of heated controversies. If indeed he was the leader of the apostles, then do his successors (the bishops of Rome) have preeminence over all of Christendom? To say that this question defined the history and the map of the Christian world for many centuries is an understatement. Saint Peter is, therefore, one of the most important people in history. And as if to remind people today that he is far from losing importance, the archeology of the last decades has revealed surprising discoveries about this apostle. Between 1968 and 1985, Franciscan archeologists discovered Peter's house beneath many layers of ground in old Capernaum. In 2013, Pope Francis displayed the fisherman's bones found in the deepest layer beneath the Vatican, thanks to excavations conducted between 1940 and 1968.

St. Peter: The Life and Legacy of Jesus Christ's Most Important Disciple examines the known and unknown about one of the most important figures in Christianity. Along with pictures depicting important people and places, you will learn about St. Peter like never before.

St. Peter: The Life and Legacy of Jesus Christ's Most Important Disciple
About Charles River Editors
Introduction
Murrillo's painting of St. Peter
   Peter the Fisherman
   A Hero's Journey
   The Rock
   Reunion and Forgiveness
   The Founder of the Church
   Martyrdom
   Quo Vadis?
   The Bones of Peter
   Online Resources
   Bibliography
Free Books by Charles River Editors
Discounted Books by Charles River Editors

Peter the Fisherman

"The violent and extreme contrasts in Peter's own nature all clearly evident. One day Peter pronounced a magnificent eulogy of Christ, the next day he sought to rebuke him. At one time we find him a companion of the master on the blessed mount, but later on we have him swearing he never knew him. Peter forsakes all to follow Christ, yet he forsakes him in the garden." - H. Lockyer

Little is known about Peter's life before Jesus' ministry, if not for a few bits of information that seem firmly rooted in history. Simon son of Jonah (Bar Jonah) was a fisherman who lived on the shores of the Sea of Galilee. Simon was a popular name at the time, a variation of the biblical Shimeon or Simeon. Peter's family came from a town called Bethsaida, whose precise location remains unknown today, but it was also located on the Sea of Galilee (also called Lake Gennesaret, north of the current state of Israel). His father was called Jonah (although John the evangelist calls him son of John), and he had one brother named Andrew. At the beginning of the narration according to Mark, the oldest of the gospels, he is working on the shore of the lake in Capernaum.

Many towns mentioned in the Bible were abandoned or destroyed, and/or changed their name or location over the centuries. It is possible that Bethsaida, Peter´s hometown, was in close proximity, an hour's walk from Capernaum at the most, since it would not be normal for a fisherman to leave his place of residence. The move probably gave Peter or his father a tax break.

There is more information about Capernaum, where Peter lived in his adult life. The site had been inhabited for at least 100 or 150 years, and it would be populated for 11 more centuries, until it was abandoned. The town was modest and marginal, of unmistakable provincial character, as archeological discoveries have revealed. Jonathan Reed, who served as square supervisor for the Israel Antiquities Authority Excavations in Capernaum, Israel, wrote, "First century Capernaum was a modest Jewish village on the periphery of Antipas´s territory relying chiefly on agriculture and fishing. In Jesus day it was off any major trade route. It was not a sought-out spot but a good place to get away from, with easy access across the Sea of Galilee to any site. Capernaum was much more modest (than nearby Tiberias and Sepphoris) at around 25 acres and 1000 inhabitants. It didn't have a gate marking the entrance to the town like Tiberias, and there weren't any defensive fortifications or walls. There were no civic structures providing entertainment such as a theater, amphitheater, or hippodrome has enjoyed by the urban elites at Caesarea and elsewhere, nor was there a public bath house. There is not even evidence of a basilica structure used either for the judicial matters, general assemblies or commercial activities. Those most likely would have been dispensed in the open areas or along the lake. The village had no constructed *agora* or market, with shops or storage facilities. Market days were held in tents or boots or on the open unpaved areas along the shore and outside private houses."

A picture of ruins of Capernaum

Fishing was one of the most lucrative trades, unlike agriculture which depends on climate. Far below on the social scale were the artisans —like Jesus— who only relied on the ability of their hands to make a living, usually as temporary workers. It is not that Peter was rich, far from it — the tax collectors working for Rome were ready to demand a part of everything he took out of the lake— but at least he must have had the means to live comfortably. He lived in a two-story house and the family had a large patio capable of gathering many people (Reed, 2001). Also, Peter and his brother Andrew had a fishing boat, which made all the difference, in that it was a means of production of great value that put the brothers above manual workers or tenants. The pair was associated with two other young people who would also become followers of Jesus, the brothers James and John, the "Sons of Thunder," as Jesus nicknamed them. As fishermen, these men were habituated in a free lifestyle, away from the crowds; by abandoning their boats and their nets they were losing not only their means of production and their share of the lake, but also life on their own terms, and in Peter's case even a wife. Perhaps there are some hints of resentment in the question he asked Jesus later in his ministry: "Look, we've left everything and followed you. What will we have?" (Matthew 19:27).

The Calling of the Apostles Peter and Andrew by **Duccio di Buoninsegna**

Around 28 or 29 AD, a prophet known as John the Baptist appeared in that region. He preached by the Jordan River. Through sources, it is known that John stirred the conscience of the people and summoned crowds to the extent that Herod Antipas had him arrested and executed in the dungeons of his palace in Machaerus, out of fear that John could unleash a revolt. Only the sight of enraged crowds scared a puppet ruler more than being removed from office for his incompetence to keep the *pax romana*.

The historian Flavius Josephus has left an invaluable testimony about John's ministry: "(John) was a good man, and commanded the Jews to exercise virtue, both as to righteousness towards one another, and piety towards God, and so to come to baptism; for that the washing [with water] would be acceptable to him, if they made use of it, not in order to the putting away [or the remission] of some sins [only], but for the purification of the body; supposing still that the soul was thoroughly purified beforehand by righteousness. Now when many others came in crowds about him, for they were very greatly moved [or pleased] by hearing his words, Herod, who feared lest the great influence John had over the people might put it into his power and inclination to raise a rebellion, (for they seemed ready to do anything he should advise,) thought it best, by putting him to death, to prevent any mischief he might cause, and not bring himself into difficulties, by sparing a man who might make him repent of it when it would be too late. Accordingly he was sent a prisoner, out of Herod's suspicious temper, to Macherus, the castle I before mentioned, and was there put to death."

Like several disciples of Jesus, Peter and his brother Andrew at some point became interested in the preaching of John the Baptist and went to see him. The New Testament gives the impression that Peter, unlike Andrew, had no patience for the threatening and apocalyptic speech of the Baptist. On the contrary, Andrew became one of his most fervent followers.

The most important disciple of the Baptist was undoubtedly Jesus of Nazareth. Although there is controversy about this aspect, most scholars are inclined to believe that Jesus was a disciple of John, and that at some point, he separated on friendly terms to start his own ministry.

One day, Jesus passed by where John was talking to Andrew and another disciple. According to the fourth evangelist, when Andrew went home he wasted no time in telling his brother Peter, busy with other things, that he had found the Messiah and that he should go and take a look at him. "The first thing Andrew did was to find his brother Simon and tell him, 'We have found the Messiah.'" Peter agreed to go and meet him. Jesus looked at Peter keenly. Mark the evangelist narrates his first exchange between Jesus and Peter differently, but both incidents are not mutually exclusive, meaning they can be two moments that connect perfectly with each other.

From the place where John was baptizing, Jesus went to the desert, where he was alone for days and then went back to Galilee. One day while he was walking along the shore of the lake, he saw Peter and his brother Andrew throwing their nets into the water. "Now as He walked by the Sea of Galilee, He saw Simon and Andrew his brother casting a net into the sea, for they were fishers. And Jesus said unto them, "Come ye after Me, and I will make you to become fishers of men." And straightway they forsook their nets, and followed Him." (Mark 1:16-18)

It is not possible to know how much time had elapsed between the first meeting of the brothers and Jesus in the Jordan and their reunion in the Sea of Galilee. Possibly it was a year —enough time for Jesus to leave the ranks of the Baptist, go to the desert, and get ready to start his own movement— or a couple of months. After visiting the Baptist, Peter and Andrew returned to work in the lake, since they had families to support and taxes to pay. Jesus found them while they were fishing. He did not stop and preach to them but simply passed by and launched a challenge: "Follow me!" That Peter and his brother left their networks "immediately" and followed Jesus makes more sense if the three characters had had a previous meeting. Mark depicts Peter as the first follower of Jesus, although this may be because his gospel is based on Peter's memories.[1]

---

[1] Several Church Fathers consider Mark's Gospel the memories of the apostle Peter. The earliest tradition comes from Papias, a bishop of the 2nd century who personally knew some of the disciples of Jesus, namely Aristion and

The Rev. and Dr. Elder Cumming, who wrote in the 19th century, once suggested that Peter required not one but three calls to forsake everything —wife, boat, family, safety— and follow Jesus the itinerant prophet, who promised his apostles, according to his understanding, that they would become part of the imminent Kingdom of God on earth. It seems safe to assure that Jesus began his ministry in Capernaum, a few miles from his native Nazareth. One of his first acts was to cure Peter's mother-in-law, who lived with him and his wife and was sick with fever. Jesus´s fame spread through Peter's hometown because he performed many miracles there. To reach more people, Jesus asked for the fisherman´s help. While Peter and his associates mended networks, Jesus climbed into Peter's boat and sailed a little away from the shore to preach. Peter was possibly returning Jesus the favor for healing his mother-in-law. When Simon finally took the call, Jesus responded with these enigmatic words: "Fear not. From henceforth thou shalt catch men." What did Peter fear? Like any person, he was likely afraid to leave behind his home and safety, not to mention the people he had lived all his life with, and his precious lake.

A Hero's Journey

The canonical gospels (Mark, Matthew, Luke and John, in that order) were completed between 35 and 60 years after the crucifixion. When the first gospel was finished, those who had known or followed Jesus were elders, and most of them had probably died. When the last gospel was completed, the apostles were distant, and each community used its own gospel composed under the authority of the founding disciple. Hence, issues such as authority and the pre-eminence of one apostle over another became thorny issues among local churches. Had Thomas disbelieved or was it an attack on his legacy? Was Paul subordinate to the other apostles or did he have authority to teach? Was Mary Magdalene or Peter the first person to see the risen Jesus? The evangelists do not even agree on the names of the 12 apostles.

It is because of these differences that historians and biblical scholars apply high historical and literary criticism to discover what really happened, which parts of the narrative are historical, which are later additions, and which simply reflect inter-community struggles. It is all the more remarkable that in regard to Peter, the agreement is unanimous - Simon Bar-Jonah was the chief disciple, the leader of the Twelve, their spokesman, and the most important associate of Jesus. It is in the details where there are discrepancies, possible embellishments, and even plain legend. Hence, a critical reading of the gospels is needed to distinguish which material is parabolic language, and which parts are likely historical. The vast majority of biblical scholars agree that the Gospel of Mark reports the facts more accurately and with less elaboration, and that Matthew and Luke used it as a reference.

In order to reconstruct the first part of Peter's biography (from his call in the lake to Jesus´s resurrection), Mark should be given the priority. This is true because he was the oldest source,

---

John the Elder. Papias asked these and other elders, and learned that Mark was an interpreter of Peter in Rome and wrote down his speeches.

and also because there are multiple testimonies that a source for Mark was the live preaching of Peter himself. Papias, bishop of Hierapolis, writing near the end of his life around 110 AD, explains how he was able to talk to the "elders," that is, preachers who had known the apostles. Papias was very interested in what Peter, Philip, John and Thomas had said, and what the living disciples like Aristion and John the Elder were still saying, and how the written gospels had been composed. When one of the elders passed through Hierapolis, says Papias, "I would carefully ask about the words of the presbyters, what Andrew or what Peter had said or what Philip or what Thomas or James or what John or Matthew or any other of the disciples of the Lord, and which Aristion and the presbyter John, disciples of the Lord say too. For I did not assume that whatever comes from books is as helpful to me as what comes from a living and lasting voice."

On the gospel of Mark, Papias says he learned from one of the "elders" (disciples of the apostles) that "Mark, who had indeed been Peter's interpreter, accurately wrote as much as he remembered, yet not in order, about that which was either said or did by the Lord. For he neither heard the Lord nor followed him, but later, as I said, Peter, who would make the teachings anecdotally but not exactly an arrangement of the Lord's reports, so that Mark did not fail by writing certain things as he recalled. For he had one purpose, not to omit what he heard or falsify them."

In order to write a life of Peter, Mark must then be given a priority. Where it leaves gaps, the rest of the gospels may complete the picture,[2] especially when they provide new material.

Next are the epistles of Paul. The book of the Acts of the Apostles may contain ancient material (Peter's speeches for example), but in general it is not considered a reliable historical source by biblical scholars.

The second aspect to consider is that the gospels contain several redactional layers. The most recent comes from the hand of the final redactors or evangelists, beneath them are older sources, and in the deepest layer is the information provided by eyewitnesses. At least from the perspective of literary theory, Peter cannot certainly be a mythological character to symbolize the perfect disciple (as could be the case with the "beloved disciple" of John´s Gospel), since all the documents of the New Testament —gospels, Acts, and epistles of Paul— agree on a consistent and far from perfect personality. Peter is depicted as a temperamental man, keen to action if somewhat reckless, loyal and sentimental, volcanic, and impetuous. He also appears as a rough, rebellious man who is violent when provoked and carries a sword. His main weaknesses are

---

[2] See the unique exchange between Peter and Jesus in Matt 17:24-29: "On their arrival in Capernaum, the collectors of the Temple tax[a] came to Peter and asked him, "Doesn't your teacher pay the Temple tax?" "Yes, he does," Peter replied. Then he went into the house. But before he had a chance to speak, Jesus asked him, "What do you think, Peter? Do kings tax their own people or the people they have conquered?" "They tax the people they have conquered," Peter replied. "Well, then," Jesus said, "the citizens are free! However, we don't want to offend them, so go down to the lake and throw in a line. Open the mouth of the first fish you catch, and you will find a large silver coin. Take it and pay the tax for both of us."

hesitation, and falling prey to fear and depression in the face of inaction. "There is more human nature in Peter than in any other of the Lord's apostles." (Lockyer, 1972)

In a certain way, the gospel could be seen as Peter's story, depicting him as the archetype of the hero. Every great episode has to do with him, particularly his actions or passivity. The Anglican theologian and scholar Richard Bauckham has convincingly exposed how the Gospel of Mark is narrated from Peter's perspective. Peter is mentioned 110 times in the four gospels, more than any other person except Jesus. Although Jesus is clearly at the center of the narrative, his personality is so blurred by so many redactional layers that it is Peter who emerges most clearly. Jesus and Peter are the two central actors of the drama, the associates who meet in the first lines of the story, join forces, undertake a journey, struggle, and have a falling out, but when everything seems lost, they reconvene again in a mysterious way, thus closing the circle. Indeed, Peter's story matches the stages of the "hero's journey" according to the literary theory of Joseph Campbell: the call to adventure (Jesus calls Peter), the supernatural aid or the appearance of a mentor (Jesus heals Peter's mother-in-law, and ordains him as "The rock"), the venturing into the unknown (the mission to preach through Galilee and expel demons), the initiation (declaration of Jesus' messianism at Caesarea), the meeting with the goddess (Peter swears to follow Jesus til the end), the temptation to abandon the mission (the failure in Gethsemane), the atonement with the father (Peter weeping at the rooster's crowing), the apotheosis (Jesus´ crucifixion), and the ultimate boon (the appearance of the risen Jesus). Finally, there is the hero´s return to bestow the boon onto his fellowmen (Pentecost and Peter´s giving the Holy Spirit). Christopher Vogler writes, "The stories of the hero always imply a kind of journey: a hero abandons his comfortable and daily environment to embark on a venture that will lead him through a strange world full of challenges." The hero grows and experiences several transformations - from despair to hope, from weakness to strength, from madness to wisdom, from hatred to love.

The Rock

From Mark´s perspective, Jesus had a resounding success at the beginning of his ministry. His fame spread throughout the region and crowds gathered to hear him preach. His disciples were numerous. Luke and Matthew (using a common source called "Q" by scholars) both mention a special commission to seventy disciples to go and preach all over Israel. In addition, Jesus gathered around him a group of 12 more trusted disciples (known as "the Twelve") who would accompany him everywhere. The number 12 has not gone unnoticed by exegesis; if there were 12 tribes in ancient Israel, by electing twelve apostles as his inner circle, Jesus was symbolically saying that the new Israel would be reconstituted around him. The different gospels do not offer the exact same list of the twelve apostles, although they agree on the names of the three pillars (Peter, James and John), and all without exception—although they show different theological interests—place Peter at the beginning of every list, an indication of his preeminence.

What then made Peter to follow Jesus? After the "new prophet" healed Peter's mother-in-law, when it was dawn and the new day had come, the fisherman realized that Jesus was not in his house anymore. Along with others who followed him, they went out to look for him and found him in a secluded place. Peter told him, "Many people are looking for you." But Jesus, instead of going back to his base of operations, where everyone would know where to go, offered an unexpected answer: "We must go to other towns as well, and I will preach to them, too. That is why I came." Jesus did not want to establish a center of power and influence, denying Peter, at whose door all the people were gathered, the chance to become a kind of broker. (Crossan, 1991). In this way, Jesus established the essential characteristics of the Kingdom movement: itinerant, un-brokered, open to all.

Peter appears in the following chapters of the Gospels next to Jesus, traveling throughout the region of Galilee and watching him perform healings, exorcisms and miracles. Jesus was not only followed by the poor and the sick, but also by the most undesirable members of society, such as sinners and tax collectors.

This was the so-called initial success stage, in which the message of Jesus —that the Kingdom of God was not only imminent, but had already begun— was accepted with enthusiasm. Stories about him began to circulate orally and the number of followers increased. The oral tradition which would later become the written sources may have been born at this stage. "A great multitude from Galilee followed Him, and from Judea, and from Jerusalem, and from Idumea, and from beyond the Jordan. And those from around Tyre and Sidon, a great multitude, *when they had heard what great things He did*, came unto Him." Jesus went back to Peter's Capernaum, performed more miracles and, plunging onto his friend's boat, began to teach a few feet away from the shore. His popularity was so great that his deeds reached the ears of his old mentor, John the Baptist.

In spite of the accusations that Jesus was a glutton and a drunkard, and that he was possessed by a demon or that he was self-centered, his fame grew exponentially. Peter (always in first place) and the brothers James and John, his innermost group, had the privilege to witness special portents such as the resurrection of Jairus's daughter and the Transfiguration on Mount Tabor. Encouraged by his success, Jesus ordered his disciples to go two by two, carry the message of the arrival of the Kingdom, and crown their preaching by expelling demons and healing the sick. When the apostles (meaning "envoys") returned, they were transfixed: "Lord, even the demons submit to us in your name."

Jesus thought the time was ready, but the Kingdom did not arrive. And the second period of his ministry, marked by failure and crisis, manifested itself. (Schweitzer, 1911). The next part of Jesus's mission was marred by controversy and confrontation. The Pharisees, the scribes and Herodians began to oppose and disprove him. On the road to Caesarea Philippi, in the northern part of ancient Israel, very near the imposing Mount Hermon of snowed peaks, Peter returned to center stage. "Who do men say that I am?" Jesus asked. The apostles began to say, "John the Baptist." "Some say Elijah, and others say you are one of the prophets." When Jesus asked his comrades what they thought, Simon had no doubts. He stood up and said: "You are the Messiah." But it is not entirely clear what exactly Simon Peter believed the Messiah should be or accomplish. At the time, the notion was not certainly that the Messiah would be God incarnate, but a triumphant king who would drive out the enemies of Israel and rule with justice. Thus, he would be like a son to God.

Peter's confession was a turning point in his career as a disciple of Jesus. Until that moment he had been a kind of spokesman, but in Caesarea Philippi, Simón Bar Jonah became the "rock" on which Jesus would build his movement. It is not necessary to be a Catholic or to discern much in order to realize that, according to all the Gospels, Peter was indeed chosen by Jesus to lead the apostles, to feed his lambs, to tend his sheep. One can imagine the scene at dusk, camping on the vicinity of Caesarea. "Then he asked them, 'But who do you say I am?' Simon Peter answered, 'You are the Messiah, the Son of the living God.' Jesus replied, 'You are blessed, Simon son of Jonah, because my Father in heaven has revealed this to you. You did not learn this from any human being. Now I say to you that you are Peter (which means 'rock'), and upon this rock I will build my church, and all the powers of hell will not conquer it. And I will give you the keys of the Kingdom of Heaven. Whatever you forbid on earth will be forbidden in heaven, and whatever you permit on earth will be permitted in heaven.'" (Matthew 16:15-19). Peter was given this extraordinary accolade from Jesus even though he did not seem to accept his teacher's understanding of messianism.

Although the narration of the incident in Caesarea has been sanitized by Matthew, it would seem that Peter and Jesus had a bitter argument about Jesus's next action. Jesus saw himself as the suffering servant who had to submit himself in sacrifice to turn the wheel of history and precipitate the arrival of the kingdom (Schweitzer, 1911). Simon, the fisherman, had a different opinion. Peter took him aside and began to scold him, which resulted in a verbal confrontation in which Jesus even called him "Satan", not a subtle moniker. Here is an account of two passionate men. In any case, the exchange reveals Peter's state of mind, and his enthusiasm at the prospect of watching Jesus in a position of honor and power, not humiliated as Jesus wanted. Karl Paul Donfried, an American theologian and Professor Emeritus of Religion and Biblical Literature at Smith College, wrote that "Jesus does not rebuke Peter for his confession of him as Messiah, but for tempting him with an understanding of messiahship that does not recognize the suffering and death of Jesus."

In spite of the disagreement, Jesus saw his friend Simon Bar-Jonah as the firmest in his faith, the most reliable of the Twelve, and the one who would stubbornly defend his cause, so much so that at some point in his ministry (according to John, when they met; according to Mark, when Peter called him the messiah), Jesus gave him a nickname. The nickname was "Cephas" in Aramaic; Petros in Greek (the language of the Gospels), and "Rock" or "Stone" in English. Although nowadays calling someone a stone could have negative connotations, in this context a stone was a symbol of a foundation and a beginning. In this metaphorical case, the rock was the cornerstone for the construction of a larger structure.[3]

The next incident that Jesus shared with his innermost group of Peter, James and John was an enigmatic experience where the four men climbed a mountain (traditionally considered to be Mount Tabor) and Jesus underwent a transfiguration. His clothes began to shine more than the sun on the newly fallen snow, and suddenly Moses and Elijah appeared at his sides, representing all the Law and the prophets. Peter proposed to raise two tents for the guests, a perplexing reaction that for the Gospel of Mark is a sign of Peter´s rudimentary understanding, even naiveté. After this Jesus began his fatal journey to Jerusalem, hoping to hasten the arrival of the kingdom (Schweitzer, 1911). On the way, sure of the fate he would meet in the city, he intimated with his trusted disciples his conviction that he would not leave Jerusalem alive.

Convinced that the group of peasants on their way to Jerusalem was following the future king, James and John asked Jesus if they could sit one on his right and one on the left side of his throne, which merited an ironic answer from Jesus, not without some disappointment and sadness for their lack of understanding. When they reached the capital of Judea, he again addressed his inner circle (Peter, James and John, always in that order) and revealed to them the imminent destruction of Jerusalem and its temple.

Shortly before this, another incident at the gates of the city would mark the fate of the movement and Jesus, something conspicuous enough to alert prefect Pontius Pilate. What happened at their arrival was so decisive that for decades it remained as one of the firmest memories of Jesus´ ministry. At the gates of the city, brimming with pilgrims from all Judea and the diaspora, on the eve of Passover - the most important holiday, when the mood was volatile and the occupation authority was on maximum alert - a large group of people received Jesus with acclamations and messianic titles.

> "They brought the colt to Jesus and threw their garments over it, and he sat on it. Many in the crowd spread their garments on the road ahead of him, and others spread leafy branches they had cut in the fields. Jesus was in the center of the procession, and the people all around him were shouting,
>
> 'Praise God!
> Blessings on the one who comes in the name of the Lord!
>
> Blessings on *the coming Kingdom of our ancestor David*!
> Praise God in highest heaven!'

---

[3] Compare with: "Jesus said unto them, Did ye never read in the Scriptures: 'The stone which the builders rejected, the same is become the head of the corner. This is the Lord's doing, and it is marvelous in our eyes'?" (Mt 21:42)

So Jesus came to Jerusalem and went into the Temple." (Mark 11: 7-11).

The cheers of the crowd about "the coming of the kingdom of our ancestor David" must have been understood as a political expectation and an inevitable warning for the ruling Romans. The atmosphere became volatile.

The reasons for the arrest of Jesus in Jerusalem and his immediate execution have been hotly debated. It is Paula Fredriksen (2012) who offers one of the most convincing explanations. Considering that other sources depicted Pilate much differently than the New Testament (both Josephus and Philo of Alexandria portray Pilate as a ruthless ruler, ready to kill en masse at the slightest provocation), it is probable that Jesus was simply at the wrong place at the wrong time, with the wrong crowd. The Romans must have caught wind of people hailing him as the son of David, which made him a candidate for king, and from there things would have been out of his hands. That Pilate seized Jesus, but not his followers, points unequivocally to two facts - Pilate knew that Jesus's movement was nonviolent and did not represent a threat (hence the Roman prefect let Peter and the others go unharmed), and that it would suffice to show the crowd their king nailed to a cross the next morning, outside Jerusalem, to extinguish their naive enthusiasm. For Pilate, Jesus's crucifixion would have seemed like the the end of the problem. (Fredriksen, 2012)

Reunion and Forgiveness

"And Peter afar off did follow him." – Mark 14:54a

Of course, for Peter, the crucifixion was not the end of the story. In fact, it was the most calamitous and decisive night in the life of the chief apostle. Although some commentators consider that the narrative of the Last Supper is a parable of Jesus's very real teaching to practice redistributive justice and radical equality, two solid facts underlie the story. In Jerusalem, Jesus was betrayed by Judas, one of his 12 apostles, and when they saw that the cause was lost, the others fled for their lives and left Jesus alone. Only Peter put up resistance. In the story, he is the hero who resists arbitrariness and injustice. Mark the evangelist writes that "one of those who stood by drew a sword, and smote a servant of the high priest and cut off his ear," but he does not reveal the man's identity. John the Evangelist, writing two or three decades later, when all the protagonists had died and there was no more danger of reprisals, reveals the name of the man who carried the sword and so vehemently reacted: Peter, of course.

The mob that apprehended Jesus took him to the house of the high priest. "They all fled," Mark writes of his disciples, but one of them went after him. Peter managed to go unnoticed in the house of the high priest, desperately trying to do something, but the downtime, inaction and fatigue took the best of him. When some maids who worked in the house of Caiaphas recognized him as one of the friends of the accused, Simon faltered. On three occasions he denied even knowing him. In a Mediterranean society where honor and humiliation depend to a large extent of recognition before the eyes of society and the people close to him, to deny someone publicly is one of the worst possible forms of contempt.[4]

Caravaggio's painting depicting Peter's denials

When Peter realized what he had done (in the Gospels the moment is marked by the crow of the rooster, as if to symbolize the awakening to the bitter reality of his betrayal), he began to cry inconsolably. In the abyss of his calling, Simon Peter cried both for himself and for his teacher. He knew that after having left everything, he had lost his honor, his program, and his home. Finally, Jesus's destiny had plunged him into disappointment; instead of establishing the Kingdom, his Messiah had died the most shameful of all deaths, the one reserved for rebels and slaves. Throughout the New Testament, Peter is the only man, apart from Jesus, who is depicted unabashedly crying.[5]

At this point in the narrative, it becomes difficult to discern among the many traditions and to know exactly what happened to Peter and the rest of the Twelve. Whatever the fate of the group, it is Peter, of all the apostles, whom the reader expects to meet again for the conclusion of the story. However, the gospels go silent after the Twelve (minus Judas) learn that the tomb was

---

[4] In the Gospel of Matthew, in the parable of the Final Judgment Jesus says that God's sentence to the condemned will be "I do not know you", that is, rejection and absolute separation.

[5] There are several references in the NT to *groups* of people crying, for the death of a child, the women in the way to the Calvary, during the crucifixion, and Paul's disciples when the apostle parts towards Jerusalem.

empty on the third day. A single laconic phrase in the Gospel of Luke lifts the veil a little; he puts it on the lips of two disciples returning from the road to Emmaus, and it shows signs of being an ancient Christian *kerygma* (proclamation): "The Lord is risen indeed and hath appeared to Simon!"

Searching further back in the history of the New Testament, around 55 AD the apostle Paul inserted in his epistle to the Corinthians what seems to be the oldest mention in history about a follower of Christ called "Cephas" (Rock): "Christ died for our sins according to the Scriptures, and … He was buried, and ... He arose again the third day according to the Scriptures, and ... He was seen by Cephas, then by the Twelve." (I Corinthians 15: 3-5).

Unmistakably, the first (or one of the first) proclamations that ran among the ancient Christians was that Christ had appeared to Peter. How did it happen? The oldest evidence suggests that it was Peter who had the original experience or post-mortem vision of his teacher. This fact is accepted even by the most liberal academics, such as Gerd Lüdemann and Robert Gundry, who have elaborated complex explanations about Peter's sense of guilt, or cognitive dissonance, that led him to experience an hallucination. Before him opened a new door of reconciliation and forgiveness, a reason to resume the Kingdom movement and a way of dealing with the hard reality. Gundry believes that Peter's original vision sparked a series of "copycat visions" among the other disciples, while the Italian Doctor Sante de Sanctis, in his book *Religious Conversion*, considers that radical conversions result from a combination of strong temperaments with a traumatic event. (Copan & Tacelli, 2000).

Interestingly, no book in the New Testament describes that special apparition to Peter, except for the very ancient formula found in Luke: "The Lord is risen indeed and hath appeared to Simon!" Paul's was very similar: "He arose again the third day according to the Scriptures, and He was seen by Cephas. "

How could the evangelists omit this foundational event of the Church, the appearance of the risen Jesus to the chief apostle? Where did it take place?

While it seems odd, it's possible the story was always there, albeit a little hidden.[6] An ancient text known as the *Gospel of Peter*, whose existence was known through quotations from the Church Fathers, was rediscovered in Egypt in 1886 by the French archaeologist Urbain Bouriant inside the tomb of a monk in Akhim, Egypt. Unfortunately, *The Gospel of Peter* is in a fragmentary state, since the beginning and end of the papyrus were pulverized over the centuries. However, the part that is preserved corresponds to the last hours of Jesus's life and the events of the first Easter. Written in the first person, supposedly by Peter himself, the gospel ends with the

---

[6] That Mary Magdalene and others had similar experiences of Jesus that they interpreted as the beginning of the general resurrection is accepted by most biblical scholars, although each one gives a different explanation of what originated these visions. A majority believes that the original vision happened to Peter.

return of the apostles to Galilee.

Sad and disappointed, they resume their activity as fishermen. "Now it was the final day of the Unleavened Bread; and many went out returning to their home since the feast was over. But we twelve disciples of the Lord were weeping and sorrowful; and each one, sorrowful because of what had come to pass, departed to his home. But I, Simon Peter, and my brother Andrew, having taken our nets, went off to the sea. And there was with us Levi of Alphaeus whom the Lord…"

At this point the story is interrupted due to the poor state of the papyrus. Everything seems to point towards an appearance of Jesus. The Gospels of Luke and John say that Peter and the apostles remained in Jerusalem and reunited with their Lord in that city, but historically it is more likely that the *Gospel of Peter* describes what really happened. After all, Peter and his brother Andrew had nothing else to do in Jerusalem. In fact they were in danger, at least of being laughed at. Why is this first appearance on the lake in Galilee not recorded in the New Testament? In fact, it has always been there, although it has been moved to different places according to the pedagogical interests of each evangelist. John´s community had already put an end to its gospel when they faced a crisis because of the death of their beloved disciple. Then they stood by a tradition they knew well, and drafted an extraordinary and valuable appendix to the Fourth Gospel. "After these things Jesus showed Himself again to the disciples at the Sea of Tiberias, and in this way showed He Himself: There were together Simon Peter, and Thomas called Didymus, and Nathanael of Cana in Galilee, and the sons of Zebedee, and two other of His disciples. Simon Peter said unto them, 'I am going fishing.' They said unto him, 'We also go with thee.' They went forth and entered into a boat immediately; and that night they caught nothing. But when the morning had now come, Jesus stood on the shore, but the disciples knew not that it was Jesus. Then Jesus said unto them, 'Children, have ye any meat?' And they answered Him, 'No.' And He said unto them, 'Cast the net on the right side of the boat, and ye shall find.' They cast therefore, and now they were not able to draw it in for the multitude of fishes. Therefore that disciple whom Jesus loved said unto Peter, 'It is the Lord!' Now when Simon Peter heard that it was the Lord, he girded his fisher's coat unto him (for he was naked) and cast himself into the sea." (John 21: 1-7)

Again Peter displayed his volcanic temperament throwing himself into the water without a second thought. The rest of the disciples came to the beach on the boat and met with Jesus, who had lit a fire to cook the fish. Then came the reconciliation between Peter and Jesus. "Simon son of John, do you love me more than these?" Peter reaffirmed his love for Jesus three times, since three times he had denied him.

John writes that this was the third appearance to the disciples, but if Jesus had already appeared to them and given them the great commission to preach the gospel, what were the apostles doing in Galilee, fishing as they had done before? Is it not more logical to think that they were again working in the Lake of Gennesaret because they believed that everything was over, and was this appearance of Jesus that sent them back to Jerusalem?

Biblical scholars also take into account the following incident in the Gospel of Matthew. Again, the original appearance of Jesus in Galilee may lie underneath. "But the boat was now in the midst of the sea, tossed by the waves, for the wind was contrary. And in the fourth watch of the night, Jesus went unto them, walking on the sea. And when the disciples saw Him walking on the sea, they were troubled, saying, "It is a spirit"; and they cried out for fear. But straightway Jesus spoke unto them, saying, "Be of good cheer. It is I; *be not afraid*." And Peter answered Him and said, "Lord, if it be Thou, bid me come unto Thee on the water." And He said, "Come." And when Peter had come down out of the boat, he walked on the water to go to Jesus. But when he saw that the wind was boisterous, he was afraid; and beginning to *sink*, he cried, saying, "Lord, save me!" (Matthew 14: 24-30).

The rest of the disciples finished the journey in the boat, and when they met with Jesus they adored him and called him Son of God. Although Matthew inserted this episode in Jesus's ministry, it may be a misplaced resurrection account. Why did the apostles, when they saw Jesus, instead of being astonished by their teacher's great miracle, cry out in terror thinking that he was *a* ghost (and thus a dead person)? Why would they ask the ghost for a proof that he is indeed their master? Underlying this narrative are the basic elements of the same story. The closest apostles are in the lake working when they have a vision of Jesus. Peter jumps into the water. Peter pleads to Jesus, and Jesus reaffirms him.

A final example to solidify the case is found in the Gospel of Luke. Luke knew the tradition of the miraculous fishing but told it in his own way, also during the ministry of Jesus: "And they came and filled both the boats, so that they began to *sink*. When Simon Peter saw it, he fell down at Jesus' knees, saying, `Depart from me, for I am a sinful man, O Lord.' For he was *astonished*, and all those who were with him, at the draft of the fishes which they had taken; and so also were James and John, the sons of Zebedee, who were partners with Simon. And Jesus said unto Simon, "*Fear not*. From henceforth thou shalt catch men." Notice the repetition of themes in the encounter between the two characters, especially the fishing motif, the fear of sinking, Peter's plea, and Jesus's reaffirmation: "From henceforth thou shalt catch men" is a commission that would acquire more meaning at the end of the Gospel than at the beginning, where Luke placed it. The key here is Peter's reaction. Why did Peter fall to his knees and beg Jesus to forgive him if nothing had happened between them? In the opinion of John D. Crossan, this narrative was originally the post-mortem appearance of Jesus to Peter that Luke modified and moved to the beginning of his gospel.

From these four examples presented above, there may actually be a single original tradition: After the events in Jerusalem, Peter and the disciples went back home to Galilee to resume their lives as they had left them. While they were conducting their activities in the lake, Peter and others saw Jesus and experienced great amazement and fear of the unknown. Peter rushed to meet Jesus, begged for Jesus's forgiveness, and had Jesus reaffirm him as leader of the apostles. Each evangelist created a different scene with the vague details he knew, but the basic plot is the same.[7]

The Founder of the Church

The Jewish historian Flavius Josephus wrote in *Antiquities of the Jews* that, although Jesus underwent the ultimate punishment as a criminal, "those who had first come to love him did not cease (to love him)," despite being considered as one cursed by God. Something happened to the apostles who once again left their boats and nets, returned to Jerusalem, and resumed the movement that their Master had started. Peter and the rest reassembled in the Holy City. It is at this moment that the sources for Simon "Cephas" switch from the gospels to Paul's epistles and the book of the Acts, written by the same author as Luke.

The book of Acts is late (written around 100 AD), as Paul's letters were composed 50 years earlier, a time with older traditions. Therefore, one must give more weight to the Pauline epistles than Luke's second volume.

In parabolic language, the Acts of the Apostles tells how the spirit of God descended upon the disciples on the day of the Feast of Weeks, or Shavuot, a Jewish celebration that takes place seven weeks after Passover. Shavuot, being one of the three great moments of pilgrimage to Jerusalem, was full of visitors from Judea and the diaspora. The disciples began to preach that day. The first reaction of the people was to think that they were drunk. Surmounting scoffing and ridicule, Peter took a step ahead, raised his voice, and took control of the situation. He was a new man.

Peter's speeches in the book of Acts constitute a material of special interest to scholars. The majority believes that they are older texts that Luke picked up and incorporated into his second volume. These speeches may answer the question of exactly how Peter began to preach when he finally came out of hiding and began the dangerous mission that, decades later, would spread throughout the Roman Empire. The message must have had this underlying pattern.

    1. Life of Jesus. "God publicly endorsed Jesus the Nazarene by doing powerful miracles, wonders, and signs through him, as you well know. But God knew what would happen, and his prearranged plan was carried out when Jesus was betrayed. With the help of lawless Gentiles, you nailed him to a cross and killed him. (Acts 2: 22-23)

    2. Resurrection. "But God released him from the horrors of death and raised him back to life." (Acts 2:24)

---

[7] Also the Gospel of Mark, which ends abruptly at 16:8, points to Peter having a special appearance of Jesus in Galilee. The angel that the women find in the empty tomb on Sunday morning says prophetically: "Ye seek Jesus of Nazareth, who was crucified. He is risen! He is not here. Behold the place where they laid Him. But go your way. Tell His disciples *and Peter* that He goeth before you into Galilee. There shall ye see Him."

3. Evidence of witnesses. "God raised Jesus from the dead, and we are all witnesses of this." (Acts 2:32)

4. Call to action. "Each of you must repent of your sins and turn to God, and be baptized in the name of Jesus Christ for the forgiveness of your sins. Then you will receive the gift of the Holy Spirit." (Acts 2:38)

The Bible contains two versions of the death of Judas, the disciple who betrayed Jesus. Both agree that it was a violent death. One of Peter's first actions was to organize the election of a new member to replace him in the Twelve. Matthias was chosen under his authority, a man who had followed Jesus too. The apostles did not leave the temple, nor did they remotely think of provoking a religious schism. They remained devoted Jews, waiting for the imminent arrival of the Kingdom.

Since the memory of Jesus being condemned to death by Pilate was still recent, people avoided to openly identify with Peter and his group, but they held them in great esteem: "No man dared join himself to them, but the people magnified them." (Acts, 5:13)

What effect their preaching had in those early days is not possible to know, but since the beginning, the Christian disciples endorsed their words with healings as Jesus had done before. Indeed, Luke attributes the first miracle of the nascent church to Peter. Upon entering one of the gates of the temple, called Beautiful, Peter and John found a man lame from birth asking for alms. When they told him that they did not have any money with them, Peter extended his hand, picked him up, and instantly the man's ankles gained strength. The beggar stood up and entered the temple with him. When people recognized that it was the same lame man who had sat at the door for years, everyone was surprised.

Peter encountered opposition among the temple authorities when he attributed the miracles to Jesus of Nazareth, and although he was forbidden to continue preaching in his name, the movement would not be checked. In a short time there was a community of faith where everyone shared their goods equally. This act was not about simple alms-giving to the poor, but about redistributive justice.

With the exception of John, the Twelve Apostles —Matthew, Thomas, Philip and the others— soon disappear from the history of the Church written by Luke, but Peter remains in the narrative throughout the entire half of the book of Acts. According to the evangelist, Peter undertook evangelizing missions to Antioch, Caesarea Maritima and Samaria. However, he took residence in Jerusalem as one of the pillars of the early Church.

Around this time, another vital figure for the expansion of Christianity appeared, one who would have great repercussions in Peter's life. A Pharisee called Saul who persecuted the Christians, that group which had already spread beyond the borders of Judea to present-day Syria, had a vision of the risen Jesus on the road to Damascus. The experience (which he himself never described) deeply reshaped his life, made him stop the persecution, and brought him to Arabia. There he underwent a dramatic conversion. After that, he went to Jerusalem, where he sought Peter and James who were (in that order) the most important Christian leaders in Jerusalem. The verb that Paul uses to describe what he did in his encounter with Peter is *historēsai*, meaning he went to ask for information about Jesus and/or to tell him about his own experience.

In his letters, Paul always refers to Peter by his Aramaic name: Cephas. They both met in Jerusalem a few years after the crucifixion, following Paul's conversion. One of the aspects that biblical scholars and historians have studied the most is the relationship between both missionaries, who eventually became the two greatest leaders of the movement. It does not seem to be a secret that Peter and Paul collided on ideological issues and that the Catholic Church may have come from an agreement between both groups, Petrine Christianity and Pauline Christianity. The information provided by the *Acts* is late, and Peter, who during the first half is presented as the main actor, disappears in the middle of the book. The second half follows Paul, as if to symbolically mark that the destiny of the Church was in Paul's hands, and no longer with Peter. At the end of *Acts*, Paul had accomplished the great mission by preaching the word of God in Rome, without interference from the authorities.

However, there is another, much earlier and reliable source of information about the relationship between both characters: Paul's own epistles. Their limitation is that they only offer one point of view. Both the pseudo-clementine literature and vague references in the New Testament suggest that Peter and the apostles continued to be devout Jews and followers of Jesus, preaching the imminent arrival of the Kingdom of God and performing healings and miracles. Paul, on the other hand, directed his mission to non-Jews, especially a group of people that the Bible identifies as god-fearers, a demographic niche between the Jews and pagans. They were not officially Jews but sympathized with that religion, believed in one god, attended the synagogue from time to time, helped to support it, and in general were favorably disposed towards Israel.

Paul's epistles also preserved bits of tradition of Peter as an itinerant preacher in the style of Jesus (I Corinthians 9: 5), going from town to town, baptizing, healing the sick and remaining in any house that received him. Several miracles are attributed to Saint Peter in the New Testament, including the following:

The healing of a lame man at the gate of the temple.

Prediction (or provocation?) of the death of Ananias and Sapphira.

The healing of the sick and possessed in Jerusalem.

The healing of Aeneas, who had been prostrate for eight years.

The resurrection of a woman called Tabita.

On these trips he was not alone. His wife accompanied him. Several of the apostles were married. Papias, a disciple of the third generation, wrote that he met the daughters of the apostle Philip. In his first epistle to the Corinthians, Paul recalls how Peter was accompanied by his wife in his evangelical mission: "Don't we have the right to bring a believing wife with us as the other apostles and the Lord's brothers do, and as Peter does?"

Paul was another kind of apostle. In the end, with the destruction of the temple in Jerusalem in 70 AD, his type of Christianity came out on top. Thanks to Paul's work among the Gentiles, Jesus's movement, looking more like a different religion, survived the destruction of Judea.

But even before those events, St. Paul met for the second time in Jerusalem with the leaders of the Church, around 49 AD. There, he reunited with James the brother of Jesus, and Peter. Subtly but unequivocally, the text notes that things had changed: Peter is no longer mentioned at the beginning of the list, but after James: "When they perceived the grace that was given unto me, James and Cephas and John, they who were reputed to be pillars, gave to me and Barnabas the right hands of fellowship, that we should go unto the Gentiles."

The order is not casual, and it signified Peter was no longer in charge of the Mother Church of Jerusalem. This is possibly because of the characteristics of his mission, because he was an itinerant prophet like Jesus, or perhaps because of internal rivalries. Either way, at some point James the Just became the most important man in the Church, and Paul became the second most important. The first letter of Clement, written around 80 AD, refers to internal rivalries against Peter: "There was Peter who by reason of unrighteous jealousy endured not one not one but many labors, and thus having borne his testimony went to his appointed place of glory."

Martyrdom

"Simon Peter asked, 'Lord, where are you going?' And Jesus replied, 'You can't go with me now, but you will follow me later.'" - John 13:37

Right in the middle of the book, *Acts* mentions Peter for the last time to be never mentioned again.[8] What happened to him?

At this point opinions diverge, but one possibility is that Peter was arrested and executed by King Agrippa (like the apostle James, the other pillar of the Church) or by the Roman procurator of Judea in functions. Among the innermost circle of Jesus (Peter, James and John), only John managed to survive until an advanced age.

---

[8] Biblical scholars are divided on the authorship of the first epistle of Peter, supposedly written from Rome. Most are inclined to believe that it is pseudoepigraphical —written in his name by a disciple of Peter when the latter had already passed away. The immense majority of the scholars reject the authenticity of Peter's second epistle.

The book of the Acts narrates the following incident: "When he (Herod Agrippa) saw that it pleased the Jews, he proceeded to arrest Peter also. Now it was during the days of Unleavened Bread. When he had seized him, he put him in prison, delivering him to four squads of soldiers to guard him, intending after the Passover to bring him out before the people. So Peter was kept in the prison, but prayer for him was being made fervently by the church to God. On the very night when Herod was about to bring him forward, Peter was sleeping between two soldiers, bound with two chains, and guards in front of the door were watching over the prison. And behold, an angel of the Lord suddenly appeared and a light shone in the cell; and he struck Peter's side and woke him up, saying, 'Get up quickly.' And his chains fell off his hands. And the angel said to him, 'Gird yourself and put on your sandals.' And he did so. And he *said to him, 'Wrap your cloak around you and follow me.'" (Acts 12:3-8).

Some biblical scholars have proposed that this story is actually a poetic narrative of Peter's death, containing several parallels with the passion of Christ to express symbolically that Simon suffered the same fate as his teacher. The apprehension occurs on the eve of Easter, but instead of having the apostles sleeping in the Mount of Olives, "the church was fervently praying to God for him." In prison, Peter is guarded by two soldiers, like the tomb of Jesus, and in the Gospel narrative, an angel is present. The heavenly being frees Peter from his chains (his mortal body), makes him cover himself with a cloak (protection), and gives orders to follow him.

The parallels continue later in the narrative. A woman runs frightened (like Magdalene) to say she has seen Peter, but her words are dismissed as idle tales by others. Peter finally appears before his companions, who are gathered in a room. His friends, who still believe him to be a ghost, see him and become amazed. Simon shows them that he is not a spirit. Before saying goodbye, he asks them to inform James (as Jesus had previously asked them to tell Peter) that he is leaving. "When he (Peter) knocked at the door of the gate, a servant-girl named Rhoda came to answer. When she recognized Peter's voice, because of her joy she did not open the gate, but ran in and announced that Peter was standing in front of the gate. They said to her, 'You are out of your mind!' But she kept insisting that it was so. They kept saying, 'It is his angel.' But Peter continued knocking; and when they had opened the door, they saw him and were amazed. But motioning to them with his hand to be silent, he described to them how the Lord had led him out of the prison. And he said, 'Report these things to James and the brethren.' Then he left and went to another place." (Acts 12:13-17).

Giovanni Lanfranco's painting *The Liberation of St. Peter*

The story carries an implicit message that Peter's departure leaves James as the leader of the church. The book of Acts says enigmatically that Peter "went to another place".

Around 90 AD, the Gospel of John, written many years after Peter's death, narrates a mysterious last encounter between Jesus and the chief apostle. The story of Jesus's first appearance to Peter may be embedded, but it also echoes about the death of the apostle. It is, without a doubt, the only authentic memory that still exists —albeit in the form of a parable— but very few details that can be deduced from the text. According to it, when Peter was an old man he was imprisoned, taken to another place (Rome?) and executed by crucifixion.[9]

---

[9] It is not unlikely. Ignatius of Antioch, considered by many historians as Peter's successor in the Church of Antioch, was put in chains and taken to Rome, where he was condemned to death to be devoured by beasts.

The scene is evocative. Walking on the seashore, alone in the cool of the dawn, Jesus speaks to Peter. "'Truly, truly, I say to you, when you were younger, you used to gird yourself and walk wherever you wished; but when you grow old, you will stretch out your hands and someone else will gird you, and bring you where you do not wish to go.' Now this He said, signifying by what kind of death he would glorify God. And when He had spoken this, He said to him, 'Follow Me!'" (John 21: 18-19). "Stretching one's hands" was a popular way of referring to being crucified.

The place of Peter's death is not mentioned in the literature of the first decades of Christianity, but by the end of the 1st century AD, there was a tradition that during the last years of his life, Simon preached in Rome and died there during the reign of Nero (54-68 AD). Several testimonies of the Church Fathers (Clement, Jerome, Justin Martyr, Papias, Dionysius of Corinth and the first epistle of Peter) relayed the belief that Peter had served as the leader (bishop) of Rome and that he had suffered martyrdom there. [10] It was in Rome that Peter dictated to Mark his memories about Jesus, as recorded by Papias of Hierapolis at the beginning of the 2nd century and Clement of Alexandria around 190 AD: "After Peter had announced the Word of God in Rome and preached the Gospel in the spirit of God, the multitude requested Mark, who had long accompanied Peter on all his journeys, to write down what the Apostles had preached to them." Before him, Bishop Dionysius of Corinth wrote around 170 AD, "Peter and Paul planted and likewise taught together in like manner in Italy, and suffered martyrdom at the same time."

The best reconstruction is may rely on historical events. In 64 AD, a great fire broke out in Rome, and for six days it caused great destruction. In search of scapegoats, and to extinguish the rumor that he himself had provoked it, Emperor Nero decided to blame the Christians for the catastrophe, since the group was viewed with distrust by the population. Romans believed that "Christians were cannibals and practiced incest. They were thought to be involved in bizarre and abhorrent religious rituals such as Thyestian feasts and Oedipean sex—the most heinous acts in Greco-Roman myth and literature." (Cassel, 1998) Thus began the first great persecution against the Church.

The Roman historian Tacitus wrote about the great fire of Rome: "Nero fastened the guilt and inflicted the most exquisite tortures on a class hated for their abominations, called Christians by the populace." He further described the manner in which they were punished, with such ferocity that the population of Rome ended up feeling sorry for them. "An immense multitude was convicted, not so much of the crime of firing the city, as of hatred against mankind. Mockery of every sort was added to their deaths. Covered with the skins of beasts, they were torn by dogs and perished, or were nailed to crosses, or were doomed to the flames and burnt, to serve as a nightly illumination, when daylight had expired. Nero offered his gardens for the spectacle, and

---

[10] Ignatius of Antioch wrote to the Christians of Rome around 110 AD: "I issue you no commands, like Peter and Paul: they were Apostles, while I am but a captive," meaning that at some point Peter and Paul preached among the Romans.

was exhibiting a show in the circus, while he mingled with the people in the dress of a charioteer or stood aloft on a car. Hence, even for criminals who deserved extreme and exemplary punishment, there arose a feeling of compassion; for it was not, as it seemed, for the public good, but to glut one man's cruelty, that they were being destroyed."

A bust of Nero

The most accepted belief is that Peter and Paul died during that great persecution. Origen wrote at the beginning of the 3rd century, "Peter was crucified at Rome with his head downwards, as he himself had desired to suffer." The story that he was crucified on an inverted cross at his own request, because he did not consider himself worthy to die the same death as Jesus, is likely not true; Nero's men, who apparently wanted to give a grotesque show, would not have taken requests from a condemned man. Crucifying prisoners in unnatural positions was part of the Romans' amusement, as Flavius Josephus noted in his works. The Church's embarrassment regarding the manner of Peter's crucifixion would explain why it was suggested Peter asked for an inverted crucifixion, while also suggesting that this kind of crucifixion of Peter truly happened.

Caravaggio's depiction of Peter's crucifixion

Both the traditions and the archaeological discoveries of the 20th century, as well as historical accounts about the site of the executions (Nero's circus), seem to confirm that Peter was crucified in a place called Ager Vaticanus or "Vatican Field", a name that goes back to the pre-Christian era. The Vatican Field was a place where dispossessed immigrants from the East dwelled. There was a cemetery nearby that was used by the immigrants. Later it was remodeled by the emperors Caligula and Nero to build the gardens and the infamous Circus of Nero, the location of the first organized, officially sanctioned martyrdoms of Christians. Tacitus wrote that "Nero offered his gardens for the spectacle, and was exhibiting a show in the circus" to placate the population. Peter, no longer the rough fisherman from Galilee but an old man willing to die for the friend he had denied, was likely martyred on the Vatican Hill. For many years there was a "trophy" (a small monument or mausoleum) to mark the place of his burial. A Christian author of the late 2nd century called Gaius left a testimony of the site: "I can show the trophies of the Apostles. For if you will go to the Vatican or to the Ostian Way, you will find the trophies of those who laid the foundations of this church."

Quo Vadis?

The Acts of Peter is a competing document which, contrary to Luke's *Acts*, follows Peter until the end, where he has a spectacular battle in Rome with a character named Simon Magus (mentioned only briefly in *Acts*). The text is saturated with legendary material, and it would be difficult to find any historical facts. However, the book, which is relegated to the category of New Testament apocrypha, contains a poignant parable about the end of Peter's life. It occurs at the end of the *Acts of Peter*, when the apostle, already of advanced age, learns that the authorities have ordered his arrest and, surely, his execution. The Roman Christian community persuades him to leave the city. At first he refuses, but he finally agrees when the brothers and sisters convince him that his presence is vital for the Church's unity.

Thus, Peter disguises himself and leaves the city, but when he is safe outside of Rome, suddenly he sees Jesus walking in the opposite direction. "And as he went forth of the city, he saw the Lord entering into Rome. And when he saw him, he said: Lord, whither goest thou thus? And the Lord said unto him: I go into Rome to be crucified. And Peter said unto him: Lord, art thou (being) crucified again? He said unto him: Yea, Peter, I am (being) crucified again. And Peter came to himself: and having beheld the Lord ascending up into heaven, he returned to Rome, rejoicing, and glorifying the Lord, for that he said: I am being crucified…which was about to befall Peter."

Annibale Carracci's painting depicting the scene

There is surely nothing historical in this narrative, except the single fact that Peter suffered the capital punishment in Rome, but parables do not have to be historical to tell a great truth. The story summarizes Peter's life in a single scene: call, failure, continuation, and ultimately redemption through example. To the Christians of Rome, subjected to cruel persecutions, the parable meant that it did not matter if they had faltered or failed like Peter; there was hope even for the one who had denied Jesus; for the man or woman who felt that she did not have enough strength to carry her cross. The story survived for centuries until this day. In 1895 the Polish writer Henryk Sienkiewicz wrote the novel *Quo Vadis: A Narrative of the Time of Nero* that was adapted to film several times in the 20th century.

By persisting in his mission to the point of martyrdom, Peter not only made sure Jesus's death was not in vain (in which case he would have to be crucified again), but also that Rome, the brutal imperial power, did not have the last word. And in order to do that, the *Acts of Peter* seem to say, the believer has to be willing to die the death of others.

The Bones of Peter

According to the legends, Peter was buried a few feet outside Nero's circus, next to the road that surrounded the building. There were already some graves on the site. For almost 250 years the place was marked by the so-called "Trophy of Gaius", which became a site of veneration. In 313 AD or shortly after that, the Emperor Constantine ordered the construction of a basilica (now disappeared) on the Vatican hill, despite the technical difficulties presented by the project. The ground was irregular and swampy, but this fact indicates that the emperor, who could have built the temple a few feet away, wanted to honor the precise place where Peter rested. In the Middle Ages, Constantine's church was demolished and replaced by the magnificent Basilica of St. Peter, the largest temple of Christianity, which remains to this day.

Alves Gaspar's picture of St. Peter's Basilica

In 1939, Pope Pius XII ordered an archaeological investigation to be carried out under the main altar to learn the truth. Antonio Ferrua, a prominent Jesuit archaeologist, led in the excavation. In 1940, the team began the search for Peter's remains under the floor of the magnificent dome designed by Michelangelo. For 10 years the crew descended through the layers of ground finding ancient coins, sarcophagi, urns and coffins from the early Christian era, unearthing breathtaking examples of religious art, graffiti and inscriptions. Under the main altar were the bases of the altar of Calixtus II finished in 1124, and below it was the altar of Gregory the Great, of the 7th century. They uncovered Constantine's monument (circa 313 AD), which in turn had been built on the so-called Trophy of Gaius, a sort of arch of the 2nd century AD which marked the place of the apostle's burial. "On one graffiti wall, amid Christian symbols and petitions, the name of Peter is carved at least twenty times, usually accompanied by prayers for the dead person, and in one case expressing joy that the deceased relative lay in the same cemetery that held the body of St. Peter." [11] An enthusiastic Vatican reported the first results of the excavations to the press and expressed its confidence that it could soon release news about Peter's tomb.

Although archaeologists found the remains of three other people at some distance who theoretically also had great importance for the early Christians, the tomb beneath Gaius's trophy was empty. But in an old 3rd century wall built in front of it, covered with Christian graffiti, which formed part of Constantine's structure, there was a single secret niche or loculus 0.77 m long by 0.29 m wide and 0.315 m high, lined with slabs of Greek marble. Inside were human bones. Monsignor Ludwig Kaas, the highest ranking person in the project and a member of the Vatican, concerned that they could be the remains of some important saint, secretly removed the bones —without telling the archaeological team— and deposited them in another place in the Vatican grottoes. This was eventually reported by the Italian archaeologist Margherita Guarducci, who replaced Kaas: "Someone (Monsignor Kaas) noticed that there were bone fragments mixed in with the plaster rubble inside the hiding-place, and arranged for these bones to be gathered up, put in a wooden box and placed in a nearby spot in the Vatican Grottoes, where they remained forgotten for a long time."

When archaeologists finally began to examine the loculus in the 3rd century wall, two meters above the Trophy of Gaius, they naturally found it empty, except for "some remains of organic material and bone fragments mixed with earth." The scientists concluded that the niche, which at some point must have contained the bones of St. Peter, had been violated in the Middle Ages and the remains had been lost. However, archaeologist Guarducci, one of the most important figures of the 20th century in her field, found the box in 1953. Beneath the ground, in a chunk of red wall Incised with graffiti inside the cavity, Guarducci found an inscription: "Peter is here." (Litfin, 2015). She immediately informed Pope Paul VI.

Guarducci had it examined by Professor Venerando Correnti, who then held the chair of Anthropology at the University of Palermo. In 1963, Correnti's team announced the results of their investigation: they were the remains of a man of strong build, between 60-70 years old, from the 1st century AD. At some time, the team determined, the bones had been buried on the ground, and later removed and wrapped with rich fabrics.

"At this point," writes the Italian scholar, "it seemed reasonable to draw the following conclusions: at the time of Constantine, after the peace of the Church (313 AD), when it was decided to arrange definitively the site of Peter's tomb, the bones lying in the earth under the Trophy of Gaius were collected, wrapped in a precious cloth of purple interwoven with gold and placed in a loculus specially made inside a wall already existing beside the Trophy. It can be added that the reason for the transfer of Peter's relics from the earth tomb to the loculus was

---

[11] Recovered on November 13, 2017, from http://www.smithsonianmag.com/smart-news/are-these-the-bones-of-saint-peter-180947833/#gLWKTRHAxeq0Tsks.99

probably the well-founded fear that the dampness of the earth, which is notoriously very considerable in the Vatican area, would rapidly damage the venerable remains." On June 26 of 1968 an "exultant" Pope Paul VI announced that investigations of nearly three decades had produced convincing evidence that the bones found under the basilica were those of Peter. "New investigations very patient and very careful, were therefore executed with a result that we, comforted by the judgement of the worthy, prudent and competent persons, believe to be positive. The relics of St. Peter have been identified in a way that we can regard as convincing. On our part, it seems obligatory to the present state of archaeological and scientific conclusions to give you and the church this happy announcement."[12]

Pope Francis I displayed the relics in public for the first time in November 2013. With a solemn expression, the first pontiff from the American continent took the small metal urn engraved with an inscription in Latin: "Tu es Petrus, et super hanc petram aedificabo ecclesiam meam" ("You are Peter and upon this rock I will build my church"), the same words spoken 2,000 years before in the Aramaic language to the ardent fisherman by Jesus of Nazareth. Like so many times in his life, Peter, the son of Jonah, the Galilean who was commissioned by Jesus himself to feed his sheep, rose again to comfort his flock.

Online Resources

Other books about St. Peter on Amazon

Bibliography

Copan and Tacelli, (2009). *Jesus' Resurrection: Fact or Figment?: A Debate Between William Lane Craig & Gerd Ludemann*. USA: IVP Academic.

Crossan, John D. (1991). *The Historical Jesus: The Life of a Mediterranean Jewish Peasant*. USA: HarperOne.

Crossan, John & Reed, Jonathan, (2001). *Excavating Jesus. Beneath the Stones, Behind the Texts*. USA: Harper San Francisco.

Eusebius & Maier Paul L. (Translator) (2007). *Eusebius: The Church History*. USA: Kregel Academic & Professional.

Fredriksen, Paula, (2012). *Jesus of Nazareth, King of the Jews: A Jewish Life and the Emergence of Christianity*. UK: Vintage.

Liftin, Bryan, (2015). *After Acts: Exploring the Lives and Legends of the Apostles*. Moody Publishers.

---

[12] Antonio Ferrua, the archaeologist who headed the excavation, and died in 2003 when he was 102 years old, was never fully convinced that they had found Saint Peter's bones.

Lockyer, Herbert, (1818). *All the Apostles of the Bible*. UK: Zondervan.

Schweitzer, Albert. London, (1911). *The Quest of the Historical Jesus.* London: Adam and Charles Black

Free Books by Charles River Editors

We have brand new titles available for free most days of the week. To see which of our titles are currently free, click on this link.

Discounted Books by Charles River Editors

We have titles at a discount price of just 99 cents everyday. To see which of our titles are currently 99 cents, click on this link.

Made in the USA
Coppell, TX
08 April 2022